The Many SINGINGS

Poems by Antoinette Voûte Roeder

apocryphile press
BERKELEY, CA

Apocryphile Press
1700 Shattuck Ave #81
Berkeley, CA 94709
www.apocryphile.org

© 2014 Antoinette Voûte Roeder
ISBN 9781940671543
Printed in the United States of America.

Cover photo by Nicholas Andrew Roeder.
Author photo by Michael Thomas Roeder.

All rights reserved. No part of this book may be reproduced, stored in a retrieval system, or transmitted in any form or by any means— electronic, mechanical, photocopy, recording, or othewise—without written permission of the author and publisher, except for brief quotations in printed reviews.

Contents

Wild Songs

The Many Singings	2
All Nature Speaks	3
Landscapes for the End of Time	4
Owl	6
Voices	7
Rant of the Powerless	8
Oil, Anyone?	9
Raven	10
Kissing	11
Victoria Harbor	12
Spring Migration	13
Raven Play	14
Heron	15
Natural Balance	16
Birthing Forests	17
Tree World	18
Lightning	19
Tree Cutters	20
Named It!	21
Starved for Trees	22
-Perhaps-	23
Magic	24
Naming Beyond Words	25
Gold	26
November	27
Change	28
Winter Surprise	29
Christmas	30
Christmas Coyote	31
Thoughts About Snow and Art	32
Kananaskis in the snow	33
A Rumor of Geese	34

Not Yet, If Ever 35
In Between 36
Cherry Tree 37
Nature 38
Rocky Mountains 39
Kananaskis Summer 40
Claims 41
Jasper National Park 42
Sometimes the earth 43
Impressions 44
Not Separate 45
Fire and Ice 46
Upside Down 47
Not a Cloudburst 48
One World 49
Last Will 50

Life Songs
Remember the Music of Home 52
North Sea 53
Amsterdam 54
The Nightwatch: Rijksmuseum 55
Rembrandt 56
Cornered 57
Doors/No Doors 58
One Hundred Years 59
Missing 60
A Second Missing 61
Peace/No Peace 62
Brahms Intermezzo 64
Geography of Home 65
Nowhere 66
The Psychologist 67
Two Ways 68
the way 69
Lessons 70

Book of Life 71
Flower 72
In the light 73
Parents 74
Women 75
Woman 76
My Mother, My Self 77
Walk 78
Idioms 79
Two Solitudes 80
Dying 81
Paleontology 82

Various Songs
The Matisse Exhibit 84
In the Gallery 85
Elisabeth's Room 87
Matthew 88
The Piano Tuner 89
Piano Lessons 91
Thairapist 93
When We Fly 95
Scooter 96

A Poet's Songs
Ten Days 98
When I write 99
Matrix 100
Life Poems 101
Un- 102
Words 103
Polyphonic Poetry 104
Grammar Jungle 105
Maybe 106
A Lifetime of Poetry 107
Trouble 108

Merwin 109
Feasting 111
Humphrey Bogart 112
Where Do They Go? 113
Wordless Poet 114

Sacred Songs
Alpha and Omega 116
Yeshua 118
Dark 119
Hallowed 120
Were you to say 121
Shema 122
Today's Creed 123
No More Questions 124
Here or Hereafter 125
The Dark God 126
Dark Night 127
Not Logical 128
Proof 129
Trust 130
Declaration 131
How Will You Come? 132

Acknowledgements 134
About the Author 136

"To be a poet is to have a soul so quick to discern that no shade of quality escapes it, and so quick to feel, that discernment is but a hand playing with finely ordered variety on the chords of emotion—a soul in which knowledge passes instantaneously into feeling, and feeling flashes back as a new organ of knowledge. One may have that condition by fits only."

"But you leave out the poems," said Dorothea, "I think they are wanted to complete the poet."

Middlemarch, George Eliot

Wild Songs

The Many Singings

"Do not blot
the many singings
that bleed into the air."

A stand of redwoods,
young ones,
planted forty years ago,
tall and strong and straight.
Already they bear the silence
of size, of ancient
history.

It is these trees I love,
that I adore, that speak
of life on earth, imperiled
as never before.

Do not blot
the many singings
that bleed into the air.

Their songs are ours.

All Nature Speaks

If everything has language
the Garry oak's arthritic branches
speak of age, the Douglas fir's
impossible height, of aspiration

The sudden thrust of a heron's bill
inscribes its hunger on darkened waters

Water's ripples tell a tale
of the earth from its beginnings

and medallions of packed earth
cry a decor of drought

All nature speaks
if we would listen
but even when we don't
this precious talk bears witness
to the aliveness of all things.

Landscapes for the End of Time
paintings by Stephen Hutchings

Remember
    the trees
    mythical beings
    many-branched
    textured with leaves
    The dappled shade
    on sandy path
    the living, breathing earth,

Earth, the beloved,
briefly held.

Remember
    the rivers
    broad and sinuous
    curving into the
    mist, mirror-glazed,
    flowing off
    the planet's edge,
    planet earth

the beloved,
briefly held.

Remember
    the seas, the sky
    as at first dawn
    when waters roiled
    and clouds bloomed
    bright and pastel shades

Remember
  the last spasm
  light unbearable
  halo of flames
  and our earth,

Beloved Earth,
briefly held, beheld, **behold**!
passes into memory.

Owl

I was awakened by a sound
so foreign, I thought it was
a dream.

"Hoot-hoot-hoot"
-short-long-short-
followed by a quick
"hoot-hoot."

I want to see you
was my silent cry.
I slipped out of bed
to the window, flung back
the drapes, gazed into the dark.

Again I heard it,
it was no dream.

I would like to have sat
and chanted with you,
"hoot-hoot-hoot,
hoot-hoot."

Voices

Do not deny
the geese their raucous call
their lively flashing
in the sun
their lyrical landings
on water.

The day may come
and soon enough
when sound and movement
and wild voices
will have
disappeared.

Rant of the Powerless

In our headlong rush
towards extinction we
pull down everything
in sight.

Trampling on the backs of
the ever-poor who have always
offered up their backs, we cry,
"More oil, more oil" while
the boreal forest swoons, falls
to its knees and ancient mountains give up
their secrets in the violence called *fracking*.

Monstrous pipelines snake through
sacred burial grounds of native
peoples as politicos line up like cardboard
cut-outs, toothy smiles congealed on faces,
hands meeting in a hearty shake for photo-ops,
while privately they revile each other,
unifying only in their wish to gut all laws
that might slow down the rape of
land and sea, the glorious head-long rush
to extinction.

Oil, Anyone?

What would you like
with it, sir, a dash
of cinnamon or perhaps

a dollop of cream
fake but oh so good?
Something else? Oh no—

we haven't had that
for months. You see

we've been monocultured
out with infestations, pests
and plagues: no grains or
potatoes and as for fish,
water everywhere is a
toxic soup and meat

depends on grains and
habitat, don't you know,
so it's just what we wanted,

isn't it, oil and oil and more
of the same. So how would
you like it, shall we try

a shake of chile flakes?
         Hmmm???

Raven

My dark feathered
friend who sounds like
ice cracking flies overhead
naming himself in bold black
strokes that bounce off chunks of
frozen sky, he being what I am not:
airborne, powerful, of great voice.

If differences form
the warp and weft,
the tender heft
of relationship, then
wouldn't we make
a splendid pair?

Kissing

My kissin' cousin,
the red-breasted nuthatch,
loops ahead of me into
the trees, making his dainty
smacking sounds, the only kisses
I will receive
today.

Victoria Harbor

The harbor master stands
tall, taciturn, midst steady
traffic of mammoth ferries
striding by, water taxis like
oversized bathtubs, seaplanes
landing heavily on plodding
feet and water, roiling and
recoiling, shaking to the shore.

The harbor master stands knee-deep
in bracken, saying nothing, directing
nothing, feathers flying,
the great blue heron.

Spring Migration

First
the sound—
distant, eerie
beyond wild

Then
the sight—
thousands of cranes
flung high upon
a deeply-clouded sky
strand after strand
in untidy waves
stirred by ancient
impulse and I
far below
shoe-shod, earthbound,
wishing for
their faithfulness,
their courage.

Raven Play

His dusky croak
cracks our eyes wide open

Two pairs of blue
seek his dark form

High-flying pirouettes
on one black wing

riding the wind,
his free-wheeling partner

We happen to see him
but with or without us

the raven's play
is its very own reason
for being.

Heron

A heron's flight
is a slow, deliberate
wave of wings,
measured, even,
pushing back
the morning.

He knows where
he is going
and what
he's left
behind.

Natural Balance

A weasel
slim, lithe
honey-hued coat
sculpted shell-ears
tail dipped in chocolate
slips out of the bush.
In its tiny jaws
a small squirrel droops
sways like a bell
lifeless.

Dreadful
Beautiful
Killer.

Birthing Forests

"I would utter forests,"
said she.

Her gaze rides lengthy trunks
tensed between earth and sky
stopped short by canopy so thick
only a mild amber light filters through
warming fall's flagrant waste of leaves,
twigs, cones, fragrant decomposed
disorder, fecund birthing bed
of a forest's progeny

and she
laboring with words,
delivered of words,
utters forests only.

For Susan

Tree World

The whole world
in a tree, each branch
a long, lingering sigh
a crooked grin
come to rest on knobby
ground, wildness wildered
into net of twigs and
leaves, a filter for
sun's grazing blaze

Aging day bleeds into
night, curves around
each feathered bush,
each pulsing life

the tree
a whole world
keeping watch.

Lightning

It exploded overhead,
so near I had to clap
my hands over my ears.

A vicious summer thunder storm
was passing, powering through.

Only later did we see the
great old poplar's trunk exposed,
semi-naked, bark stripped off
without mercy, ruthlessly,
blonde moist skin ripped open.
Later still, like a wounded martyr,
the skin ran rivulets of pink and red.

The poplar's trunk was charred and at
its roots the ground revealed
a small black hole, entry point
of the electric charge. Shards of bark
lay willy-nilly as if a giant
had been playing.

A giant, ruthless, without mercy,
Mother Nature in her least mothering role.

Tree Cutters

What was it like,
you red-plaid men,
armed with saws, ropes,
pulleys, to surround
the giant redwood standing
in its agèd grandeur
surely rooted in the earth and
rising, ever rising, clad in
furrowed, frowning, brown-stained
bark, crowned in a finery of needles?

What was it like
to take this mighty spirit down
till it lay broken at
your steel-capped feet?

At the end of the day
did you go home
tired, proud,
satisfied?

For Emily Carr and Edward Bertynsky

Named It!

After I have examined
the leaf bracts and the cones,
pronounced it an alder,
the book closes on my mind.

The tree in all its
lively leafiness
is identified, boxed up
for future reference.

No more will I wonder,
no more will I quest.
My eyes are shut
to alder-ness. I named it,
it is done.
The mystery
is gone.

Starved for Trees

Starved for trees,
she says, as they wander
beneath an autumn awning
of spreading cottonwoods,
russet maples, broad-leaved
catalpas with their snaky seeds,
trees so big they meet at their crowns,
their trunks a giant's armful.

She comes from a far-north climate
where days are short. Trees work hard
to root, to grow to any height, never quite
achieving the majesty of their cousins to
the south.

The luxuriant foliage and size
resemble a banquet and only now
does it dawn on her that her diet
has been an anemic one. She has been
starved for trees.

-Perhaps-

a currant bush, perhaps
a gooseberry, scalloped leaves
in shades of cherry, copper,
peach, more beautiful in autumn
than any one I know
and quieter. I want

to lie among these cushy
bushes, "to sleep, perchance
to dream", perchance never
to wake up again...

Magic

Hunkering clouds brood
and scowl erasing mountains
with ease. Nasty winds
ply their trade. September
chills chase the leaves. When

we brave the bluster, walk
in wetly-scented forest,
clouds pull back, lift their
pregnant bellies and the magic
they have been hoarding blazes
brilliantly from summits that
should never be without the
startling beauty of fresh snow.

Beyond Words

Dollops of snow
drop heavily, splay
in the sun's powerful
glare

A spruce grouse startles
out of the brush
with a great
hullabaloo
of wings

Before this moment
cracks, splits off into
another let me name

the blessing-blue sky,
the grounded gold leaves,
the deer cutting a swath
between trees, the trees our breath,
my breath driving my life,
my life in this moment
blessed beyond words.

Gold

Climbing up this rocky trail,
falling behind the others,
one late aster pokes through
the grass, back-lit by
an ever less amicable sun
that moves us inexorably into
winter's grasp yet on this last day
of October illuminates the lavender fringe
and holds it in a bubble
of gold.

November

Indifferent
dull and
deafening grey

It slumps between
October's festival of
colors and December's
abundant snows

It's neither this nor that
and way too long

Can't we just get rid of it?

Even the calendar
might be grateful.

Change

Winter was a nocturnal thief
that dawn found out. It left
behind a rock-hard lake
dressed in a thick white coat.

Its lively water stilled,
its sharp reflections stifled,
its wild chop erased.
Moribund and taciturn
it stood with nothing of note
to catch the eye.

I had forgotten
from winters past
the advent of wind-sculpted
waves of snow, glittering crystals
evoked by the sun, the scissors-shaped
tracks of the hare, the paw prints of
a some-time coyote.

Once again I need eyes
willing to welcome the cold
stark land, invite its beauty
like the returning friend
it is.

Winter Surprise

Surprise in winter sometimes comes
in the form of a bouquet of birds
swimming in a monochrome sky,
swarming waxwings, plump
little birds, small conformists
erupting from the crowns
of poplars or the dense skirts of
spruces, with an occasional stray
slipping away and promptly
flitting back again.

They swirl, they whirl
as if components of
a textured flowing
and if you stop
to watch a while,
bundled and bulky in
parka and boots,
you may see them
spread out above you
like a blessing, feel yourself
becoming lighter, lifting off
to join them in their ephemeral
terpsichore.

Christmas Eve

One tall, slender tree
with a crown of scraggly branches,
leafless now for several months,
reaches for the remaining cup
of sunlight offered by a star
descending quickly to the dark
embrace of the horizon on this
last day before Christmas.
Its trunk glows amber
for a moment till it too
is found by shadows long
in winter, ready to enfold it,
shadows longing for profound
deep darkness into which they'll
melt in ecstasy appropriate for
this holy night.

Christmas Coyote

I open the drapes
on Christmas day
and there he is
struttin' his stuff
at the end of the lake
and up the hill.

Does he know it's Christmas?
That in neighboring houses
folks are clambering
out of bed to open gifts,
or sleep it off from the night before
or sick, like you, with fever and cough?

He is the coyote
out in the snow,
free of schedules
and expectations
and heading into
the ravine.

His Christmas gift,
the one that is his
each day of the year is
the whole wild wonderful world.

Thoughts About Snow and Art

The sky has forgotten
what blue is.
The ground
only knows snow.

In between
a fine mesh screen
of swirling crystals
day after day.

It is like a painting
by Seurat, the only difference
being his brushes were wands
of light, his palette a plethora
of color.

Kananaskis in the snow

but the sun is pressing through,
and Mt Kidd reveals one shoulder
then another through the clouds
and clouds are moulded mounds of
whipped air moving in such stately
fashion, slipping over lip and rim
of mountain. Snow drops straight
like a beaded curtain, icicles plunge
from eaves along the roof, water
trapped in long slim spears.
Pines troop darkly, every branch
festooned with tongue of snow,
snow heaped up on needles bunched
like shaving brushes dipped in cream.

It is altogether delicious,
not a soul is in sight,
just the whitely cushioned landscape,
silent and demanding nothing,
undisturbed but for one bold
black raven cruising by and my
loquacious gaze.

A Rumor of Geese

Sometimes when I am seated
on my meditation cushion
I think I hear their nasal call.

Meanwhile winter spins
its crystals and a bright
new sun sends sparkles
off the snow.

I hear them, though I know
it isn't so but at this moment
are they dreaming of
a blue and endless journey,
silent ribbon of starlit nights?

I hear their faint
and ghostly honking,
hear them thinking
their return:
"We are coming,
 we are coming,
 we are almost on the way."

Not Yet, If Ever

Late April Easter
and still the lake
stands stubborn with
ice, mangy old ice,
stained and certainly
past due.

So surely think
the disconsolate geese
plodding across
yet one more time,
squatting down as if
on a bed made
of silk.
A mallard couple
waddles past, knows better
than to set up house...
not yet.

We plod and waddle
and wish away
the heaps of dirty snow
still stacked on north-facing slopes
wondering whether this year
resurrection will finally fail.

In Between

A snow storm in spring
gauzy swaths
unleashed in the east
gathering momentum
masking perimeters
slathering white
on white
with the exception of
a disconsolate crow
pecking blackly
at the base of a spruce
and a hapless gull
tossed up and sideways
on obstinate gusts
of crushing wind,
both given over
as am I

riding the cusp of
the in between.

Cherry Tree

Underneath my window stands
a tree dotted with blossoms
frothy puffs of pink petals
just emerging, a tree

bursting to be full,
to be gorgeous, to express
its tree-ness on this city
sidewalk, the most ego-less
of voices calling,

> *Don't miss me,*
> *look at me,*
> *look at me!*

Nature

pulls out all
my stops. I become
a soapbox speaker
all my senses in overdrive,
stretching language till it snaps,
plumping words like sofa cushions,
putting paint on Van Gogh's canvas,
dollops textured and twirling wildly,

so excited
so engaged
so delighted
am I once again
to be alive and
in this wooded
mountain-scape.

Rocky Mountains

I am wedded to
the Rocky Mountains

they who do not yield,
are anything but gentle and

so bold, one would never pick
a quarrel with their constancy,

maturity, their presence in
the morning and throughout

the hours of darkness. They
seduce me with their colors,

shades of dress depending on
the sun or cloudy cover and

the trees that leap
upon their slopes,

that spring out from
their canyons.

I am wedded to the mountains,
call them my beloved bridegroom.

Kananaskis Summer

This sky
copious container
of blue and white

This mountain
silent giant of
grey granite

Over and above
before and behind
wherever I turn
their great embrace

I am such a pagan.

Claims

Siesta time has claimed the
mountains. Kidd broods over
the valley, scowly in
the heat. Up ahead,

beyond the yellow warning
a black bear and a grizzly
occupy their terrain and we,
we turn around,
retrace our steps.

No arguing with bears.

We have been accompanied
by violets, purple surprises,
bright white strawberry blooms,
the nodding caps of yellow dryads
and always the blue clematis,
starry petals dropping, creeping
up on anything that will have it.

Forbidden today are the meadows
filled with shooting stars and prairie smoke.
Perhaps the bears cavort among them.
We give way to their commanding presence,
to their prior claim.

Jasper National Park

Before I leave I want to see
once more the snowfield
on the Opal Hills

black bear weighty
on its paws
lumbering slowly
up a cliff

a grizzly
knee-deep
in turquoise river

an eagle on its nest
its white head a beacon
across Medicine Lake

the bejeweled loon
slipping under water
smooth as oil

These I acknowledge
These I salute
once more before
I leave and pray
they never vanish
from the earth.

Sometimes the Earth

Sometimes the earth
is too much for me.
When my eyes are too finite
to bear the image of granite peaks
thrust up from lush meadows, when
the scent of piny forest after rain makes me
want to drop to my knees, when the grandeur
and the majesty push my breath back down my throat
stopping, starting, stopping again, then the earth is too much
for me, with me, in me and I gladly give it back,
loose its hold upon me, hand it over
to the universe to keep within
its grand embrace.

Impressions

Surging, boiling, splurging,
sometimes merely sneaking,
coiling around this massive
mountain, clouds
start their trek
across the valley.

What cauldron holds
these eruptive beings,
what powers them,
where do they sail?

Catch one, fly it like
a kite, or even better,
mount it, ride this beauty
through the sky and from your
cloud-ly perch behold the jagged
earth beneath as it unrolls its carpet
painted many colors, any of which
would put the Impressionists
to shame.

Not Separate

When rain started falling
so softly I could not be sure
whether I was still sleeping
or I had become by some silent
alchemy the rain itself. Black
blotches of cloud rode a charcoal
sky moving toward dawn and in
this timeless time when nothing
had yet separated out, sky, rain, and
sleep were all the same.

Fire and Ice

Fire and ice
at the world's edge

deep crimson and mauve,
a tinted duvet
flung upon sky

Water turns lilac
on the lake while fire
on high grows, glows and clouds

too white for eyes,
sculpted icebergs
strain at their moorings

anticipate
the daily eruption

Upside Down

At dawn the clouds
fell into the lake
and lay pristinely
on the bottom.

The spruces formed
dark smudges, growing
head first from
the clouds that
had drowned and
no matter how

I tried to set
things right, every
thing insisted on
its topsy-turvy
way that day.

Not a Cloudburst

The sun came up
unknown to us
this morning
as sky scowled
huddled close
dripping, leaking
an intimate refrain
close as an embrace
accompanied by
grumbling,
low and sweet.

Not a cloudburst.
Not this time.

One World

A quiet morning
and the houses line up, upside
down, chimneys and balconies
a flawless reflection on
the lake's smooth skin.

A small pack of clouds
drops by for a visit,
a jet's vapour trail
snakes a path in the
water and I look up
to the very same scene.

There is but one world.

Last Will

I want to draw
my last breath in
a stand of trees
aged and weathered
sun slanting through
  wind tossing
    leaves stirring
      birdsong slipping
down muscled trunks
Somewhere above
a woodpecker's wild cry
the drum

    drum

        drumming

                dying

                        away

Life Songs

Remember the Music of Home

Memory casts her silvery net
over meadows crisscrossed by waterways,
skies thatched with wings of windmills,
every horizon abrupt with spires,
cradle of our dim but growing awareness

when the weather cock cried us awake
to short winter days crammed into desks,
walking home in the near dark bundled
up in heavy coats and sensible shoes

summers when we bravely built
castles and moats on the beach though
the sun broke through but rarely
and cardigans covered our swimsuits

One endless day we boarded a ship
and sailed away with only an echo
of what we had known, an orchestra
suddenly silenced.

Much later, on foreign soil
memory refocused
and what was lost
was found to be the music
that had never stopped playing.

For my sister Joan

North Sea

Gulls rise from the sea like rain on
the wind, the restless sea
typically grey,

seagulls surfing the waves
more gracefully than
any human, rocking back

and forth in constant motion,
foam cresting whitely, insistently
beneath, one wave stumbling

on another from here to the unchallenged
incision where earth and sky meet,
the untranslatable North Sea of
my native land.

Amsterdam

Sunday morning coots
make their ablutions
at the confluence of
five canals. Unperturbed
by a slim sleek boat
that silently plies the
opaque water, still less
interested in two stately
swans riding regally by
I have to wonder whether these
ducks are aware of the graceful
arched bridges they swim under
or the historic facades of ancient houses
once belonging to wealthy merchants?

The coots I know are little tugs,
swarming the prairie lakes of western
Canada under a vast open sky.

How different
how different life is
for each of us depending
on where we swim.

The Nightwatch: **Rijksmuseum**

    Rembrandt van Rijn,
    the Mozart of painters,
comes through the headphones
loud and clear: a lecture on how
and why and what he painted.

    Everyone stands
as if mesmerized, ears attuned
to the disembodied voice. My head
unencumbered, I stand weeping,
    shot through the heart by
    his golden light.

Rembrandt

van Rijn, that clever fellow
paints with light and shadow
not with brushes,
brushes have been laid aside
for folks with lesser gifts.
Instead
we see the means of soul
the tools of spirit.
Four hundred years later
we fall into his web,
anointed with
the painter's gold.

Cornered

This moment is nailed
with past regrets

The walls decipher
our distorted shadows

We crouch in a corner
of our lives

Its broad weave rolls away

Tapestry
never
retrieved

Doors/No Doors

One door after
another shuts
with an echoing
clang as the world
recedes
or is it I
who drop a little
at a time
out of time.

With each door
the distance grows
the hollowness yawns
like an open tomb
till I'm a mere speck
at the tunnel's end,
foreign to you
unknown to myself.

When next you look,
will I be there?

One Hundred Years

My life
is more than I can bear
at times.

When I get stuck
on the same round-about
that spins me into the past

I am lost
awash in grief
hopeless, helpless
to change a thing.

It's all done now
but what is done
is written on every
cell and sketched onto
your soul

and mine. All I can bring
to it now is love,

love for you,
love of self

and still
I could cry
for a hundred years.

Missing

I did not know
I had been missing
until I began
to show up.

Decades were strung
like paper dolls,
flimsy white cut-outs
all linking arms—

a suspension bridge
over a chasm so deep,
so dark, I dared not
look down.

I spent years joining others
presenting the person they
wanted to see, hiding
me.

Showing up feels so
precarious, but the dolls
are gone and the chasm reveals
a wandering ribbon of water
dappled with sun.

I am here.
Despite my fears
I put one foot in front
of the other and risk being
who I am.

A Second Missing

I did not know
I had been missing
until I began to show up,

put one foot before
the other on that bridge

that hung precariously
over a pit of vipers, coiled
and writhing, waiting to nip
my heel, strike my ankle.

Taking that first step
is possible though not
easy. Following through

is the snake-pit,
the old familiar tendency
to abandon self to other,

you, on the other side,
me, gone from here because
I have been waylaid
by the snakes.

Peace/No Peace

Peace to you
this night I said

but where is it
for me?

At 3:00 AM the peasoup
I enjoyed at lunch

plays hide-and-seek
inside and thoughts

have gone astray
in the nocturnal world

bounce off every hushed
and shadowed bush

sit with you my friend
who sits with her husband
who labours for every breath

sit with the pit I dug
for myself in an otherwise
innocent conversation and

wonder how
I'll meet my commitments
since I've forgotten

how to sleep and if
there is peace to be had

this night it has forgotten
me.

Brahms Intermezzo

It starts with a question
that lingers throughout
a minute and a half of
music, ruminating,
rumbling, building not
to a climax but
a fluid embrace
ending with a sigh,
not an answer in sight.

Brahms' Intermezzo Opus 76, #4

Geography of Home

Towels whirling
in the dryer

You are practicing
your sax

The promise of
a cup of tea

This is the map
of home

Nowhere

at home. But the quest
never ends. Nowhere

at home. Try to persuade
yourself that you are

free and therefore every
where at home. Then finally

one day when you are way
past middle age and musing

under the shower, water
warming up reluctant joints

and crabby back, it comes
to you. Nowhere at home,

of course, because it's not
a *where*. Home is essence,

seed stock, root, the deepest
self, the unfathomable spark

we are and never are
without.

The Psychologist

Every two weeks
she sits opposite
the psychologist

on a couch too soft,
too deep for comfort
or perhaps for truth?

Together they pull out
the strands that glitter,
clamor for attention.

Others fall away, fall
back into the fabric,
just as worthy

of regard but somehow
overlooked. They form
the weft and weave of

daily life and in the end
are what remain to be
lived out.

Two Ways

She did not have that much to say
until the second half of life
when she learned to translate,

translate heart to head,
as everyone knows,
the only accepted idiom.

Between these two
ways of being lay
a train crash, a shipwreck:
high water, twisted steel.

Between the two,
soul was crushed,
was drowned, its
language lost and what
had been alive, died.

I do not think much
of eternity. If it means
more of the same
I shall not volunteer.

the way

Now is the time
to plod on through
the dreary days of
late November into deep
and utter darkness, groping
for the way that is unknown
yet waiting to be forged,
created with each step until
in breath of spring-light we look up,
look back, can say, "Ah, that is what it was:
the way."

Lessons

Hiking uphill in the Rockies,
terrorized by fear of bears,
brown and grizzlies, thirty years
of fearful hiking.

Years and years of rowing
pulling mightily on oars
upstream against a righteous
current. Learning how to

face the wall, to find a
foothold, scale it, never mind
the scars and bruises, isn't that
what walls are for?

Learning how to pick up, go on,
persevere, create a hopeful
peace and comfort, learning,
learning, sick at last of

learning from another's text
and striding out into the world
to be oneself and *un*learn
fear.

Book of Life

It seems as if
I hear you say,
this chapter has no place
in this book. There ought
to be a law, a code that regulates
such things.

This book is not a box.

When it falls open
it reveals
pages still uncut,
harboring words yet
unread; and look, is
that the end or has
the bookbinder been careless,
see those pages, loose and
flying off in all directions?

Perhaps this book
knows no censor.
Perhaps it is
all-inclusive,
in the end, never finished.

Life is so untidy.

Flower

I'm blooming differently now...
not so much fragrant sweet peas
fluttering like moths but sturdy
sunflowers big of heart, dark
and prickly, rich with seeds.

I'm not going to let you pull
me down out of season.
I will feed throughout winter
birds that come for my seeds

and you can choose
to be one of them
or not.

In the light

In the light
of forever
your *yes* and my *no*
mean less than the
arch of your eyebrows,
the part in my hair.

In the eternal now
they are the truth
of discipleship.

In the light
of forever you and I
are hung out to dry
between heaven and earth
until we become transparent

just a few threads
that the wind bears away.

Parents

They've been dead
some twenty years.
Still I fill the
air waves with
their names, dictums,
values, words.

>Exit stage left.
>Empty the stage.
>Here come the ones
>who *really* matter.

In the shower's wet cell
(a wisdom retreat)
I hear different words:
  in your 70th year
  it's time to heed
  your voice, value
  your own experience,

  celebrate the gift
  of you and pass
  that on, not the
  painful powerful
  ghosts of the past.

Empty the stage.
Enter stage right.
Take your place.

It really matters.

Women

I wish you had talked
to me of men or maybe
more of women, you
a woman, I the same.

My female awareness
was formed by father,
brothers, boyfriends,
teachers, doctors, by
a husband

     not
by woman's knowledge
of her luscious bodily self,
her depth of soul, her intuition,
her sometimes dangerously
compassionate heart.

It has been such arduous labor
carving out a place for myself
and such a lonely and beleaguered
road, I wish you had talked to me
of yours and shone a little light
my way.

   to my mother

Woman

A female knows
right from the start
what it is
to have her legs

pried open by
a doctor or a
lover—to have
her body taken over,
 ever after to be
shared, to give up
what was sovereign,
never to belong to herself alone
again.

Who am I then, *whose* am I
then? What are *my* rights?
What can *I* ask?

Years go by,
they still persist,
those questions, as she
looks back at a girl who
seemed to know her boundaries
once, knew herself
undivided.

My Mother, My Self

Walking by a mirror
is a sobering affair
these days and sometimes
when I do, I hear myself say,
"Is that *you*? I had forgotten."

More often it is
my mother I see,
her blue-grey gaze
not yet dimmed by
Parkinson's sculpted mask;
her pleated lips, a string bag
gathered at the neck; vertical
lines descending at the corners
of her mouth drawn into folds
by gravity's inexorable pull.

Instead of drowning in despair
over resilient skin forever gone
I am so glad to have
my mother back
if only in a mirror.

Walk

My hair bounces
off my neck
as it did
when I was eight.

I wear the forest's warmth.
Its fragrance breathes me.

The body in all its
fullness, ripeness,
comes along—with its
buds and bruises,
folds and tunnels and
fanciness.

When I find my rhythm
the weighty way of each step
connects me to gravel and sand
beneath my feet and my hips
shout alleluias, joyful to steady
my swaying frame. Surely

embodiment, of all gifts,
is the greatest one.

Idioms

There are languages
only the hands know:
the white and black tuxedo keys
of the piano, the slip and slub
of silk, crisp paper and the heft
of a pen, the smooth contour of
bread dough,
every crease and cranny of
your blessed body.

I speak them all.

Two Solitudes

      Sunday morning walk
      Holiday weekend
      Strangely quiet out

      Between every footfall
      an eternity

I see you inert, sedated, umpteen tubes
and wires connected to your body, swollen beyond
recognition, fluid build-up despite dialysis

      Another footfall
      more eternity

I see your brother sitting at your bedside
calm, steady, holding your hand

      When did I ever
      learn to walk?

I see your wife bending over you.
"Can you hear me, sweetheart?"

      Why is this so difficult?
      One foot comes down while the other lifts off
      yet I seem to be getting
      nowhere.

      Is that how it is
      for *you*?

For Dave, Nancy, Michael

Dying

As he lay dying
he was heard to say,
"Tomorrow I'm going
to meet my Lord."

As my mom lay dying
I was told she asked,
"When am I going
to heaven?"

Is it a who?
Is it a where?

When death comes riding
my horizon,
what will I
be able to say?

Paleontology

Some day
will someone find
an imprint of
a woman in
the multi-layered
earth, next to
species long extinct,
ferns and trilobites,
delicate fishes, spiraling shells,
will someone
find
me?

Various Songs

The Matisse Exhibit

Tunneling up
into an oatmeal sky
the art gallery forms
a glass wormhole
a rivering spiral of
fluid dizziness.

Hard to focus
on Matisse.
He is focused
on female nudes.

Bombarded by breasts,
bellies, bottoms, buttons,
indistinct hands
block-like feet
I'd be happy to take
a slow boat to China
or just to step out
in Alberta's white winter
where people, thank goodness,
are dressed to the nines,
every inch covered up.

In the Gallery

It is my second time
with these paintings

twice in one day
overcome by their spell

I sink to the floor,
back to the wall

enter each life-sized
canvas, washed by muted

light, sepia tones, dark
shadows, luminous sky

and trees, trees,
water, water

Paintings to live
and die by, be
resurrected to.

Two women wander by,
chat about style,

chronology, location, a
not unpleasant murmuring.

When silence falls, I see them
sitting pertly side by side

headphones on, eyes riveted on
a video flickering
on the wall.

Ever so small, the seductive video,
found in every museum now.

It moves, we follow,
leave behind the muscled, personal
presence of the art surrounding us.

These wall-sized paintings
apparently static
may leave some hungry
for more. For me
their beauty is as much
as I can bear.

Elisabeth's Room

Welcome to Elisabeth's room:
small yet spacious
clean angles, clear surfaces
sober, simple and congruent.

Above her single bed
a wall-sized picture shows
a rope bridge slung over water
disappearing in the fog, an
archetypal tree with wraith-like
branches beckoning in the mythical mist.

The invitation is yours
to stay or
step lightly
into the picture
onto the bridge.

Can you resist?

Welcome
to Elisabeth's room.

Matthew

Then there is Matthew,
tousled toddler, bold explorer,
standing on the verge of the great Pacific,
eager to impart to me
the treasure he has found,
the mystery of a sandal
left behind on the muddy beach.

Want to come and see? he asks,
ready to slip his hand in mine.
(What treasure is *that*?) I give
his request a passing thought
and loath to step into the mucky
mud, I ask instead
about the milk-white puppy
sitting on his mother's foot.

The moment passes.
It starts to rain.
Matthew turns away
and I have missed
the adventure of his hand in mine,
the blessing of his trust.

The Piano Tuner

He strides in on
a frosty morning,
toolbox in hand,
neat little mustache
perched on his lip,
his brown eyes lively
with anticipation.

What can he fix
for me today?

He opens my grand,
a big black bird,
angles its wing
towards the sky
and sits down to
a shower of notes
the brilliant, key-traversing
arpeggios only a tuner
shakes out of his sleeve
with so much gusto.

He works diligently,
electronic box on the floor
winking beside him, the
tuning fork having long ago
joined the annals of antiquity.

A couple of hours pass
and he reports that he has
fixed the blubbering of the

action and what's more, has
sugar coated the tone.

I visualize the delight of
Christmas baking, cookies
and puddings that melt in the mouth.

Eager to taste my "new"
piano, I let my fingers stray
over the keys. It is like slipping
into a bath: the tone is mellow,
the action so smooth it comes to meet me.
Rachmaninoff sounds both
creamy and muscular, as
he should.

My tuner has slipped out
the door, check in hand,
but look! listen! to what
he left *me*!

Thank you, Vince.

Piano Lessons

She was beautiful—
small, slim, quick
and eager, oh so eager
to learn.

Week after week
she sat at my grand
with fingers wrinkled from
repeated washing. She'd
struggle with notes she had
not had time to learn after work,
after household chores.

Then one day she had no car.
Could I come to *her* house
for the lesson?

I drove across town
through tree-lined lanes
that gradually gave way
to small sober homes.

Her house was bare
but for a few sticks
of furniture, the queen
bee being the old upright.
Out of a back room came
tumbling two boys, giggling,
embarrassed, and I the only white
person there.

We sat together on her bench
while music struggled
into the room.

There was never another lesson.
She never came back.
I never heard
from her again.

Thairapist

"Hair-apist," says Joanne.

The mirror reflects
our knowing grins.

Her gifted fingers
work my hair.

I visualize
a handsome plaque

posted strategically
by her chair

where all her clients
eventually land,

spilling their lives
with each snip of the shears

often accompanied
by tears.

We trust Joanne,
her compassionate heart,

her thoughtful words
and in the end

we prize her hug
at least as much
as the skill with which
she dresses our hair.

When We Fly

The vacant stare
of the waiting lounge,
people who've left
their bodies behind
or never occupied them.

We've all submitted to the system,
shuffle-sigh-surrender,
security's suspicious searches,
to the endless snaking corridors,
the funnelling tunnels of a maze
ending in a tube with wings
that violates the skies.

With luck we will arrive
at our dream destinations,
creaking and unfolding, and
repeat the pattern in reverse
retrieve our bodies with our bags
at the baggage carousel.

Scooter

Who would have thought
that I would be tempted
to write a poem about
a dog? I had been scared
of them since I had been
attacked by a German shepherd
trained in Vietnam to go
for the throat. Thankful to say
his aim was off, settling for
a chunk of my thigh.

Scooter is the happy result
of the blissful marriage,
undoubtedly, between a
cocker and a schnauzer
and goes by the somewhat
unfortunate label of *schnocker*.
He has won my heart.

He prances on a dancer's legs,
wears a comely beard and a black
curly coat. When he looks at me
with his milk chocolate eyes
I am entirely his.

Alas, he's not mine. But this is
fair warning, (don't you agree?)
to the owners: you've heard of
"a thief in the night",
haven't you?

A Poet's Songs

Ten Days

Ten days, every day
a sky as white
as earth below
with constant traffic
in between of
powder and pellets
flurries and flakes
pouring down like
a beaded curtain or
swinging from east to
west along an uncharted
plane.

And I could give in
to despair, being snow-
bound-embraced-enveloped
but focus instead
on the traffic that
swirls up from inside
that begs for paper
and pen, intending
poetry.

When I write

I want to crawl so deep
that time eclipses
and I live again
what I have seen.

More than that
I want to join it:
feel the earth's pulse;
split the water
with the loon,
look through his
red eye; rush
over boulders, chat
with beached stones;
embrace the valley
from my snowy summits,
lay my self bare
beneath the sky,
breathe the thin air
and gaze forever
into the blue
or turn into cloud.

There are no limits
when I write.

Matrix

A writer
a poet
is by vocation
witness
and observer.

How else
to write *about*
some thing?
One surely has
to stand away
to see the whole.

Some day I want to write
from the epicenter of the earthquake
from the core of the volcano
from the crest of the tsunami
from the human heart whose passion
knows no map or location.

Could I do that
and survive?

Life Poems

I learned early
to keep my own counsel.

When louder voices
shouted me down

I retreated inside
and dialogued there.

Life grew hugely
in the interior

until it found
a pathway out

in the lilt and line
of poetry.

I ride the rhythms,
cultivate cadence,
listen for music
and breathe,
and breathe.

In just such a way
inner knits outer
into congruent whole.

Un—

If you, like I, believe
that poetry reveals its essence
in the porous texture of each word,
in the white space in between and
the tremulous breath at the end of
a phrase, then you, like I,
believe in the poesy of
the un-said.

Publishers and literati
like the volubly obscure, viscous
mounds of verbiage to wade through,
arcane references to legend and myth.

You and I with our bare bones poems,
a few words followed by one gorgeous exhale,
will be left un-published, un-marketable
and predictably,
un-read.

Words

Music was once the radio's domain.
Now it is talk and banter,
rude remarks, over-familiarity
and rap.

The age of technology has brought us
e-mail, facebook, twitter and tweet,
blogs (rhymes with bogs),
nothing to do with letters
thought out carefully,
written in a graceful hand

nor does twitter refer to birdsong
and facebook is more talk.
Midst all this claptrap,
brouhaha and confabulation
it is incumbent upon the poet
to pare down language to fewer words
and light them up so they leap off the page.

Polyphonic Poetry

Three o'clock in the morning,
proverbial witching hour,
and I awake to rumors of,
what *are* they, coyotes?

I slip out of bed, dragging
my afghan to keep me warm
in the cool cave of the living room.

Grebes, our slim red-necked
friends. The two arrived just
yesterday to claim their former
home on the lake. Now
their shrill and jagged cries
cut like a jigsaw through
the night, intersect with
the rumble of a passing train.

Earlier, a different sort of
serenade: three poets reading
at a book event. Now their cadenced
ponderings accompany the love song
of two ducks over the quiet nocturnal
waters in the out-of-time dreamscape
of 3:00 A.M. and who
the real poets are
is not at all
clear.

Grammar Jungle

The poet hunts verbs
wading through swamps
oozing with adjectives
articles racing down
spiny trunks of
intertwined trees and
swinging through broad-
leaved canopy, conjunctions
grinning wickedly.
Adverbs dog her heels
as she hauls her feet,
one by one, out of the
literary goo, glares
at grammar, grabs pen
and paper, sinks with relief
into poetry.

Maybe

Read sky.
Forget words.

Not even poetry
approximates gazing.

Maybe a woodpecker
rockets by, shimmering
red on your retina.

Maybe a jet's trail
weaves your vertebrae,
spine spun against the blue.

Maybe a wind
casts clouds aside,
tumbling, crashing,
lightning flashing.

Maybe your life
is written in sky.

A Lifetime of Poetry

We poets may begin
with lyrical phrases praising
nature's beauty, its diversity
and end up after many years of
slogging through the human swamp,
with dry and disappointed protest,
short and bitter proclamations.

Somewhere in between
there may appear
a glimmer of reality.

Trouble

The Trouble with Poetry is
it engenders more poetry
as Billy Collins freely admits.

I read the above and
am prompted to request
five or six books by Billy
with titles like *Sailing Alone
Around the Room*.

He fantasizes about
a painting on the wall,
the ivy wallpaper behind it,
the mice nesting in the wall,
the concrete crumbling around them
        and
is named to the illustrious post
of poet laureate of the United States,
the President's right-hand man.

I read him with a frequent giggle,
with an occasional sigh.

I see why.

The Trouble With Poetry, collection by Billy Collins

Merwin

W. S. Merwin writes in stanzas
sometimes alternating rhyming
lines holding to eight syllables
he has no need for punctuation
he can tell a story fifty
pages long with never a pause
I cannot put the book down not
for breakfast nor for sleep the tale
continues at full throttle

his life story is woven through
most every poem and must
have been a sad one there are few
occasions for celebration
he loves the earth and history
that is clear to see *Lament for*
the Makers is a poem naming
poets known to him who have since

died it does not include a French
derelict called Villon whom he
learned to read in the original
tongue he talks repeatedly of
views from windows from a sixth
floor walk-up from a farm on the
river Billy Collins likes his
window views and come to think of

it so do I as a matter
of fact all poetry is surely
the view from the poet's window
be it literal or that of
the soul

    Big Breath
    Full Stop.

Feasting

Saturday morning and
it is still dark
when you go to market.

You hobnob with farmers
and feast on the sight
of pumpkins and squash,
potatoes and peppers
and come home laden,
flushed with delight

while I dig down deeper
into our bed and enter the garden
of Kunitz's poems. I wander its paths,
peer through branches, stumble (nearly)
on luscious late roses that startle
the senses with redolent blooms.

We each have our feasts.

Humphrey Bogart

In the black void
of early morning
sleep is a stranger
skulking down
deserted streets in a
crumpled trenchcoat
hat shoved down over
gaunt lined faced
a Humphrey Bogart
stepped out of time.

When this shadowy prowler
lurks on the sidelines
of dreams I could
be dreaming
all I can manage
instead of sheep
is to switch on the light
and read my way
into somebody else's world.

Where Do They Go?

Where do poems go
in winter?
Do they button up
in overcoats,
hunker down in
mufflers,
struggling down
the avenue,
braving
the north wind?

Or have they fled
to tropical climes
to lounge on beaches
palm trees swaying
overhead and I,
wishing I were there too?

Wordless Poet

The poet lives
between
the words, or rather
dives into and out
lives the open
spaces, breathing
always breathing
into the next
turn of phrase.

What she would prefer to do:
record her breath, leave no mark
no trace
a blank page
a break

in
the air

Sacred Songs

Alpha and Omega

In the beginning
was the word
and the word was
Fire. From it

sprung chaos
which expressed
itself in spinning,
spiralling and space.

Then came bodies
of all sorts, hard, hot,
microcosmic and beyond
measure. Finally
we appeared, our
bodies soft and
hard, hot and cold,
pliable and un.

We discovered fire.
We made fire.
We caused fire,

created so much chaos
that the spinning, spiralling
planet stopped in space,
reversed itself and....

In the beginning
was the Fire.

The end was
as the beginning.

Amen.

Yeshua

He said, pick up
your mat and walk.
Be with my people.
Bring bread.
Share bread.
Be bread.

He did not say
build me an altar
get on your knees
worship me

nor did he say to
climb the mystical
ladder of ascent
enjoy the lofty company
of angels.

No.

So I walk this uneven
ground, mat in hand,
cast my lot with the
wounded and weary,
the ill, despondent and
the broken. This I know
to do.

Dark

My dark and silent God,
you dwell within me,
knitted into me. When

did you climb down from
those icy heights and decide,

no more separation? When
did you consecrate,
anoint my body and my
senses, the dark presence of
my breath, as yours and yours
alone?

Hallowed

I no longer haunt
the hallowed halls of prayer
looking for you.
You are not there

anymore than you are
to be found in earth or
sky yet in all of these
more present than our feeble
words can say, therefore in me
as well.

There is no separation
here or there, out or in
with you.

Were you to say

"There is no God,"
and pile up notes,
treatises and texts
to prove your point,
I would smile.

Were you to say

"God is all powerful,
all knowing," with
one hand on the Bible,
the other upon the mystics,
I would smile.

But were you to say

"I have no words,
I know nothing,"
and stand before me
empty-handed and surrendered,
I would smile, embrace you,
call you kin.

Shema

My friend professes God
but has no faith.

Every morning
every night he prays
what he's been taught
by rote. The holy Hebrew
scriptures roll off his tongue
like wine but he himself tastes
nothing.

Faithless
he is
faithful.

The "Shema", Jewish prayer spoken upon waking and just before going to sleep each day, comes from Deuteronomy 6:4-9.

Today's Creed

I do not know *who* God is.
I do not know *what* God is.
I do not know *whether* God is
but I choose to live
as if Love were the source
the weft and the weave
aware of the opposite
and holding the balance.

No More Questions

I have ceased my
endless questioning
refuting your existence
or translating from heart to head
whoever, whatever you are.

My yearning,
the longing that cries
for you is my comfort,
my assurance.

If I dwell
in perfect illusion
it is no matter.
You are
what I desire.

Here or Hereafter

What if eternity
were here and now?

What will you do
with the words of regret
you have saved for your mother,
gratitude for your aunts,
forgiveness for your father?

Time to love
to argue
to forgive
right now

What will you do
with eternity?

It will take care
of itself.

The Dark God

lets his rain fall
on the good and bad alike.

Innocence is violated
every moment everywhere
on earth.

Prayers ascend from
the mother of the murderer
and the murdered,

from the tortured, lost
and drowning
and the deathly ill.

If we are made
in the image of
God and each one
has a dark side,

what about God?

Dark Night

Some time after
you have been kissed by God
and the sweet signs of love
are all in the past
and plodding is
your daily bread

acceptance moves in
recognition rearranges
the furniture
and every ordinary act is
just what it is
imbued with Presence.

Not Logical

Logic will not
show the way.

Reason won't
provide a map.

Some things can never
be explained.

The heart's flight
the spirit's dance
take place somewhere
beyond our ken

can only be sensed
perhaps described
by poetry and paints

not with
the machinations
of the mind.

Proof

I am letting you off the hook
    God

You don't have to prove you love me
by turning the red light green
by curing a friend's cancer
by stopping all torture, war,
human stupidity, natural disasters

by giving me back
the years when I could not
trust much less hope
in order to live them again
and this time
better

I will not ask for proof.

You are.
I am.

It is enough.

Trust

When trust has set you
free, even prayer takes wing,
releases its urgent needs.

Let go your prayer for the world.
In the vastness of each breath
all the world presents itself
and *you* are not apart from
them. Your desperate pleas
echo down the corridors of
the mind like a doubting child's
to its preoccupied parent.

Is that trust?

Trust is freedom
to let God be God.
When you fully inhabit
your breath
it is your prayer.

Declaration

If ever there is to be
a declaration before a
higher power, some thing
that would sum up
a life, my words
would have to be,
"I loved your earth."

How Will You Come?

How will you come for me
Beloved?

Will you come with kisses,
royal robes,
with pain and struggle,
lingering lament?

Will you part the fibers
of my chest and scoop
my heart to yours?

Will you smile upon
my soul, call my spirit
home?

How will you come for me
Beloved
and

will I come
willingly?

# Acknowledgements

The following poems were published previously in *Sageing: A Journal of the Arts & Aging, with Creative Spirit, Grace and Gratitude*. This is an online journal, a publication of the Okanagan Institute, Kelowna, British Columbia.

"My Mother, My Self"　　　volume 13, fall, 2014

"Remember the Music of Home"
as "Remember the Music"　　volume 12, summer, 2014

"Landscapes for the
End of Time"　　　　　　　volume 11, spring, 2014

"Missing"　　　　　　　　　volume 6, winter, 2013

"Second Missing" as
"Missing (2)"　　　　　　　volume 6, winter, 2013

"Kananaskis in the snow"　　volume 6, winter, 2013

"Nature"　　　　　　　　　volume 6, winter, 2013

"Not Logical"　　　　　　　volume 5, fall, 2012

The quote that begins "Birthing Forests" is taken from a poem by Susan McCaslin called "Caliban", first published in *At the Mercy Seat:* Ronsdale Press, 2003.

"Perhaps", with apologies to William Shakespeare.

Profound thanks and appreciation to Nicholas Andrew Roeder for his photograph and design of the beautiful cover for this book.

Author photo by Michael Thomas Roeder.

About the Author

ANTOINETTE VOÛTE ROEDER has a Master of Music degree and a certificate from the Pacific Jubilee Program in Spiritual Direction. She is a poet, writer, and spiritual director in Edmonton, Alberta, Canada. Antoinette facilitates prayer and meditation and leads retreats in the areas of poetry, spirituality, and mysticism. She is passionate about the Sacred, music, people, and the earth. Her previous volumes of poetry, also published by Apocryphile Press, are *Weaving the Wind*, *Still Breathing*, and *Poems for Meditation: An Invitation to Prayer*.

www.ingramcontent.com/pod-product-compliance
Lightning Source LLC
Chambersburg PA
CBHW031136090426
42738CB00008B/1105